MW01341281

A Guide for the Prophetic Scribe

Tokunbo O. Okulaja

WAKE FOREST, NORTH CAROLINA

© Copyright 2022 - Tokunbo O. Okulaja

All rights reserved. This book is protected by the copyright laws of the United States of America. This book may not be copied or reprinted for commercial gain or profit. No copies of this book or any parts of this book can be reprinted or disseminated in any form including-electronic, mechanical, photocopy, recording, or otherwise unless you have prior written permission from the publisher- TTL Publishing. Permission will be granted upon request.

A Guide for the Prophetic Scribe
TTL Publishing
P.O. Box 1744
Wake Forest, North Carolina 27588
info@tokunbotheleader.com

Visit the author's website at tokunbotheleader.com.

Cover design by Darius Carr.

Unless otherwise noted, all scriptures are taken from the New King James Version of the Bible.

A Guide for the Prophetic Scribe/ Tokunbo O. Okulaja. 1st edition
ISBN: 978-1-7378576-8-6

CONTENTS

Chapter 1: 26 Signs of a Prophetic Scribe 1

Chapter 2: Responsibilities 7

Chapter 3: Activations.. 15

Chapter 4: Growing Your Prophetic Scribe Gift 23

Chapter 5: Prophetic Scribe Protocol............................ 33

Chapter 6: Increasing Your Creative Intelligence................. 39

Chapter 7: Prophetic Scribe Roadblocks 45

Chapter 8: Hardships of a Prophetic Scribe..................... 57

Chapter 9: 27 Prophetic Scribe Declarations 63

Encouragement for Prophetic Scribes 67

Notes 69

About the Author... 71

Introduction

What is a prophetic scribe?

One of the gifts that God has given us is the ability to hear His voice. As Believers, we should all be able to hear God's voice for our own lives. God has given us the gift of prophecy where we can hear a message or a prediction from God that can help us in every season of our lives. As prophetic scribes, we also have the ability to help other people navigate through life by providing them with a message from God.

Nebuah is a Hebrew word that refers to prophesying. There are different ways that one can deliver a prophecy. Prophecy (a prediction/message from God) can either be spoken out loud or written down. (See 2 Chronicles 9:29). First, a prophetic scribe has a strong gift of prophecy. All Believers have the opportunity to prophesy, but prophetic scribes should consistently be able to retrieve prophetic messages from heaven. Prophecy is meant to bring edification, comfort, encouragement, and correction to the listener. The role of a spirit-led writer is to intentionally hear from God to write down a message or create work that will bring His people warning, edification, comfort, and encouragement.

A message from the Lord can come in the form of having a word of knowledge. A word of knowledge includes having current facts about someone or information about someone's past. When you have a word of knowledge, the Holy Spirit then gives you more information as to how this past or current fact affects this person's future. Prophecy can also be a word of wisdom, which is receiving a solution from God. In addition, prophecy can include events that will take place in the future. (See 1 Corinthians 12:4-11). Messengers from the Master learn how they best receive information so that they can help others learn what heaven is saying.

All prophetic scribes are messengers who are anointed or called by God. They receive an agenda and mandate from heaven to be His recorder here on earth. A prophetic scribe means that a person can navigate with the Holy Spirit to write down a message that comes from Him. They may go into a writing project thinking one way, but as they maneuver through they can easily sense, feel, and hear the Holy Spirit shifting them into a different direction. Because this is a gift, it is easy for these messengers to pivot as they write with the leading of the Holy Spirit.

A prophetic scribe may find it easier to write down prophecies versus speaking them out loud. Of course, prophetic scribes have the ability to use their voice, but they receive a flood of information and put it in writing for many others to read.

Being prophetic does not mean that someone is a prophet, but it means that this type of scribe or writer can easily partner with the Holy Spirit to write down messages that He wants disseminated to His people. A lot of prophets can enjoy writing eloquent messages for God's people. Because prophets have to hear God's voice, it is natural for them to use their writing to warn and encourage His people.

Individuals that write with the Holy Spirit understand that what He wants to be recorded in the earth realm is more important than being popular or on "trend." The key to being a prophetic scribe is mastering being led by the Holy Spirit. A spirit-led writer hears what God wants to say in this hour so that His people can move towards their destiny and live an abundant life. Spirit-led writers do not have to fully understand grammar, punctuation, or language rules. They are not intimidated by what they do not know; therefore, they keep on writing for God's glory. These messengers with pens understand that language mechanics are important, but they place priority on hearing God's heart so that they are motivated to continue writing for Him.

These messengers with pens are not typical scribes because a traditional scribe mostly focuses on writing what is said by another person. The direction that a typical scribe receives is from man, but the revelation that prophetic scribes receive is from God. The Master is truly the conductor of the pen, and He uses man as His vessel to move the pen.

Some examples of prophetic scribes obviously include the individuals that played a part in writing the Bible. Apostle Paul is a well-noted contributor to the New Testament. It is said that he wrote about 13 books in the Bible. His messages were focused on helping church leaders navigate through Christian living and engaging the culture. Prophet Isaiah (and many others) in the Old Testament had a hand in declaring the prediction and birth of the Messiah. God used the prophets in the Old Testament to delineate what should be expected surrounding the events of the birth of the Messiah. Their writing was passed from one generation to the next to be used to study the Savior that was to come in the New Testament.

Focus

Spirit-led writers are focused on giving people clear definitions of what God has called them to do in various seasons of their lives. There are specific concepts that the Lord wants His people to understand in certain seasons. Spirit-led writers help bring to remembrance or to the forefront what the King wants His people to focus on. These writers are charged with hearing directly from heaven so that His people can focus on their identity, purpose, and destiny in Christ.

In addition, there are authors that are gifted to write on certain topics that God is concerned about His people understanding. There are prophetic writers that have been given revelation, wisdom, and understanding on ideas that the Church needs more information on. Prophetic scribes can expound upon unique topics to give the Body of Christ more clarity, instruction, and insight in these areas. For example, there are some anointed writers that are gifted to compose a series of books on finances, relationships, prayer, etc. An anointed writer has immense knowledge and wisdom on certain subjects and is able to partner with the Holy Spirit to give His people more information on these topics.

Writing Projects

God can give you different ways to express your writing gift. As you grow with God, He will give you various writing assignments to complete. Being God's writer means that you can use your gift to give people personal prophecies. You can also write down visions for groups of people that speak directly to their organization or community.

In addition, you can be a vessel to help write a general blog post or articles that will impact various groups of individuals. Your prophetic writing gift can lead to writing books to expound upon information that will help His people live successfully. You may be gifted to write commercials, movies, tv shows, curriculums, speeches, podcasts, scripts, poems, and/or plays that have God's perspective.

Ultimately, as God's scribe, you should help Him present information that will lead others into transformation. Seek His face for how He wants to use your prophetic writing gift. Do not limit yourself to how your skill set can be used. People's perspectives are shifted through the use of media, language, and rhetoric. How far you want to go with your writing gift is dependent upon how much you invest in becoming better at your craft. If you believe in the multidimensional nature of God, He can use you in multiple ways as a writer. As a spirit-led messenger, you are multifaceted. Never become too familiar with your writing gift. Becoming familiar with your writing gift will cause you to not take the time to seek out your uniqueness as a scribe. When you seek God's face on how He can continue to use your writing in different spheres of influence, you become a writer that can create without limitations. Allow God to use your writing skill to impact the world.

Chapter 1

26 Signs of a Prophetic Scribe

The following are indicators that God may want to use your pen to deliver a message to His people. You may not have all of these signs, but you have a strong desire to grow in these areas. A budding prophetic scribe should have at least five of these signs. It is your responsibility to invest your time and resources to evolve in using your prophetic scribe gift.

1. **Holy Spirit-led:** These individuals create outlines and visions for what they want to write, but they can easily sense the direction that God wants to go in. When they feel the new direction that God wants them to go in, they can shift into this direction with great ease. They are more concerned about what is on the heart and mind of God when it comes to their writing. They understand that their words have weight and meaning when they choose to allow the Holy Spirit to be their guide with their writing gift.

2. **Series of Books/Writing Topics:** You may receive one book idea, but when you start working on this idea it triggers the idea for another book. This person receives an exhaustive list of ideas to write about based on the same topic. For example, this person can have a whole series of books about marriage because God has given them the

volume and grace to write on this topic. It is not uncommon for this person to possibly be writing three books at one time. In addition, this person may create a blog series on marriage ideas because they are full of information that God wants His people to hear.

3. **Free Flow:** We can always find you writing something short or long. You can easily sense what God is saying and naturally start writing it away. You may be a person who has an overflow of used-up journals because of the amount of time you spend writing with the Holy Spirit.

4. **Relevant Revelation:** What you write is still relevant years later. Sometimes you read something that you wrote 5 or 10 years ago, and you can still find that it is relevant today.

5. **Weighty Words:** The words you type bring conviction and sobriety to readers about what God says about them. Your words activate people to be excited about moving forward into the plans that God has for them. In addition, people believe what you write because you represent a Being much higher than you.

6. **Bible Nerd:** You are a person that loves the scriptures. Not only do you love the scriptures, but you are also interested in helping people thrive by way of incorporating the scriptures into your writing work.

7. **Researcher**: You have an area of focus that you do extensive research on. You have an interest in certain topics and do what is necessary to know the many facets of this subject.

A GUIDE FOR THE PROPHETIC SCRIBE · 3

8. **Note-taker:** You are always found taking notes in a meeting. It is not difficult for you to transcribe what a speaker says. In addition, you are meticulous and organized when it comes to note-taking. You have a note-taking system that helps others to follow along.

9. **Linguistics of Heaven:** You have the ability to give people definitions and language about what God is doing in their lives. When people come to you, you give them vocabulary so that they can understand the season that they are in. It is your desire to hear fresh words from heaven so that you can help other people to thrive in their season of life.

10. **Silence is Solitude:** Silence from outside noise is important to you because you want to track what God is saying. You place a high priority on listening to God's voice. You can hear God's voice when you take time to turn off outside noise.

11. **Wisdom Giver:** One way that you heal from horrible experiences is that you extract wisdom from less than favorable moments. You retrieve this wisdom so that you can help other people to heal and thrive in their life.

12. **Action-Oriented Writer:** Your writing inspires people to take action. You desire to use your words to inspire people to take action in their lives.

13. **Obsessions:** You may be obsessed with having the perfect journals and pens to write with. A fresh journal or pen gives you excitement.

14. **Language Lover:** Your soul leaps with joy when you hear and see how writers beautifully construct words. You are careful with your word choices because you are a lover of language. In addition, you are obsessed with learning new words and using them in your writing.

15. **Devotion is Important:** You enjoy time with God because it is in these moments that He gives you the wisdom that could only come from Him. You understand that your prayer life is important to stay connected to what God wants to say to His people.

16. **Healing Through Writing:** You experienced healing through writing about your pain; therefore, you have a strong desire to help other people learn how to use writing to heal. You want people to understand the freedom that takes place through writing about painful moments that they have endured.

17. **Poetry:** You may have an interest in poetry. You may enjoy writing poetry that causes people's perspectives to shift. People can feel the power of your words in their souls.

18. **Sing Your Song:** You have the ability to sing out the words that you write. Some call you a songwriter. You have the creative intelligence to put a melody to words on paper.

19. **Abstract Ideas:** Ideas that may seem disconnected to others can easily be related by way of your writing gift. You have the ingenious ability to creatively put words and

concepts together that may not seem related to the average person. People are intrigued by how well you caused different concepts to mesh well together.

20. **Writing Over Speaking:** You know that you are called to speak, but you feel much more comfortable writing down God's message. When someone asks you for something, your first inclination is to write it out.

21. **Social Justice:** Writing is a tool that you use to bring awareness to issues of social injustice. You believe that your words have the ability to confront formidable foes that oppress people in society.

22. **It Came to Pass:** Part of the gift of prophecy is writing out predictions. Test to see if what you write comes to pass.

23. **An Expert:** You are well-versed on a topic, and you can write extensively on this topic. You have an unusual amount of information on a topic that can help transform other people's lives.

24. **Idea Generator:** Your writing can be used for podcasts, tv-series, lives, coaching programs, etc. You have the creative intellect to use your writing in more than one mode of communication.

25. **Practice What You Write:** Sometimes you will have to live out a hard message before you get to write about it. You write messages that you have lived out. Oftentimes, people experience healing because your message was potent because you lived out the message. You find

healing in being able to share the story that has been given to you.

26. **Prayer:** You use the scriptures to create prayers that will help yourself and others live victoriously. You write out declarations and proclamations to teach people how to pray the will and Word of God.

Chapter 2

Responsibilities

There are a few responsibilities that prophetic scribes must understand that they have when it comes to writing for God. As was mentioned before, a writer led by God is not an average writer. The type of work that you are called to write is meant to highlight what God wants to say on the earth. As a messenger, you have the responsibility to seek God for what He wants to see written. Writers led by God document what people need to hear. They also educate people by giving them language and definitions for their destiny. Writers led by God are called to bring direction, clarity, and focus to people.

Hear from Heaven

Before you start a writing project, it is best to ask the Holy Spirit what He wants you to create. This should also be practiced when you are posting something online such as a Facebook status, blog post, or any other post on social media. Proverbs 3:6 NKJV states, "In all your ways acknowledge Him, And He shall direct your paths." It is your responsibility to discover what it is that God wants to share with His people. If you seek Him first, you should never run out of ideas or information. Seeking Him first also gives you access to explore the genius mind of the Father.

Hearing from heaven is a skill that you are going to have to learn how to practice as you grow with the Lord. There are different ways that God can speak with you. It is between you and the Holy Spirit to discover how God wants to convey His messages to you. God can speak to you through visions, dreams, numbers, pictures, words, etc. Figure out the best way God communicates with you so that you can navigate with Him when it is time to write out what it is He wants to express on the earth.

When He delivers the message, it is your duty to bring it forward so that others can read what God has for them. You take the symbols, visions, dreams, pictures, concepts, etc. that God has shown you, and you make it plain for other people to understand. If you simply state what God showed you, and you do not share the practical meaning, it will be difficult for others to understand it. You have to figure out how to articulate in words what God has shown you so that others can apply it to their life.

Those that are intentional about growing in the gift of prophecy often receive moments where God challenges them to hear Him in a different way. Do not get frustrated when it seems like the Master has shifted how He wants to communicate with you. There are times when some messengers get too dependent on one side of God, but He wants to show them more about Him. In each season, discover the different modes of communication that God wants you to become familiar with. These are invitations for you to mature in your gift of prophecy, which will help you become a greater creator. When you graduate from one method, He will continue to challenge you so that you can first learn more about Him and then second evolve in your abilities.

Write What People Need to Read

Oftentimes, you can dilute God's message by not being authentically you. It is important that you write what heaven has given to you to express. You forfeit the ability to be powerful when you try to write on topics that are popular or on-trend. If you have not been given the grace to write on a certain subject, do not speak on that topic. You will sacrifice the impact that God wants to make if you write something that is not authentically you.

In addition, you may be charged with writing on a topic that you do not feel that confident writing about. You may feel unqualified or uncomfortable writing on certain ideas. If He continues to bring it to your attention daily, then you may need to consider what it is that He wants you to document. God wants you to write material that is going to mature other people.

Sometimes you do not have the luxury to write about what you feel needs to be documented. Do not allow yourself to get carried away with trying to satisfy your own creative ambitions that you lose the heart of God's message. There is always room for creativity in God, but you cannot only think that every message or idea that He wants you to write is something that is going to feel good to you. God is only going to give you what people need to read, especially if it is a direct message to a person or an organization. One of the ways to make sure that you write what people need is to use the following checklist.

1. **Scripture Test:** Test to see if what you wrote is something that can be found in scripture. If what you are writing is something that can be found in the scriptures, then it can be a message from God. Ask the Holy Spirit for scripture to justify what you write. This is the best way to analyze and test the veracity of the messages you receive from heaven.

2. **Repetition:** Another test to confirm that this is God speaking is that later on, you hear trusted voices in the body of Christ saying the similar message that you

already wrote down. After you have written what God gave to you, you may hear other trusted spiritual mentors speak on that similar subject. (Please do not go seeking this confirmation. It should naturally happen.)

3. **Father's Nature:** Is what you are writing related to the heart and nature of God? You have to study the nature and character of God to understand how He would speak. You have to ask yourself: Does this sound like something a Father would say to His children?

4. **Redemptive:** Even if what you are writing is a difficult word, what you write should also bring hope for the future. God brings correction, but He also gives His children hope to breakthrough after receiving correction. In addition, be careful when giving personal words of correction to specific people in higher seats of spiritual authority if you do not have a personal relationship with them. If God wants you to send them a message, He will grant you open doors to these people. The area of rebuke and correction is typically the responsibility of high-level or seasoned prophets with great authority. A beginning prophetic voice should use caution and discernment when it comes to writing words of correction or rebuke to others.

5. **Freedom in Wisdom:** Is what you are writing going to give people a solution to a problem? If you are discussing a problem in your writing, ask God for a godly solution that will break weights off of people. Part of prophecy includes a word of wisdom. 1 Corinthians 12:8 conveys, "for to one is given the word of wisdom through the Spirit, to another the word of knowledge through the same Spirit," (1982,

NKJV). If you are writing something that details a problem, ask the Holy Spirit to give you wisdom from His heart to solve the issue. If the solution brings freedom to the listener, then this can be a message from the King. In addition, there will be freedom in wisdom because the person may be motivated to have the faith to see the solution come to fruition.

6. **Increase in Faith:** The words that Spirit-led messengers receive should help individuals increase their faith in certain areas of their lives. Where someone may have not believed God for something, your words will help increase their faith. They will partner their faith with doing work.

7. **Peace:** Test to see if what you are writing brings peace to you and the reader. If writing the word seems like too much human effort and striving, then you may want to keep the word to yourself until you feel a 100% release from God.

8. **Warning:** In addition, your written work can be from God if it leads people into suffering for the sake of becoming more like Jesus. Sometimes, you will be tasked with delivering a message that will forewarn someone about the suffering that is to come. Ultimately, the message on suffering should still always point back to drawing closer to the Father.

Providing Language and Definitions

One of the greatest parts of being a prophetic scribe is being able to hear the right words that can help people understand their identity, assignments, seasons, purpose, and destiny in God. There are people who need clarity about where they are going. One of the ways people receive clarity is by way of them understanding times and seasons. The Father gives prophetic scribes the acute ability to understand times and seasons. He gives you the vocabulary to give to others to explain certain schools of thought or seasons that people may be in. You can put what you learn in any written work such as books, articles, screenplays, etc. for many others to experience.

A biblical prophetic scribe that gave people hope in the midst of a season of great suffering is Apostle Peter. Apostle Peter brought comfort to the many churches that he supported by way of giving them information on how to navigate in the time and season that they were in. For example, when the church endured intense persecution, Apostle Peter gave them the language, vocabulary, and definitions on how to handle the arduous times that they were in. His words in 1 Peter and 2 Peter helped the church to understand the benefits of the present suffering that the church would have to endure. In addition, his words gave them the language that was necessary for them to understand how that season was going to bring glory to God.

There are people that are going through difficult and joyful times. By listening to the Holy Spirit, you can provide people with the words that are necessary to help them withstand the journey that they are on. There are individuals who prematurely quit a process because they do not have enough clarity and direction on how to maneuver through that season. Think about how many times you have said to yourself: I wish someone told me that when I was going through _____. Sometimes, you say to yourself, I needed this message years ago. Think about how you felt when you received more information about who you are called to be. Remind yourself of how elated you felt when you found out the linguistics of heaven that directed you into your destiny.

God has given you the terminology and concepts that will help His children break free from addiction, poverty, stagnation, cycles, and so on. Allow Him to use your pen to bring His children the information that is necessary for them to thrive in the Kingdom. You can help people thrive by providing them with the right information. The right information is people having the ability to articulate what season they are in and receiving definitions in life. God's people have freedom when they have the correct vocabulary to navigate through life.

Your Pen Brings People Focus

Prophetic scribes have the duty of announcing what the King is doing on the earth. Writers led by God relay to people how He wants them to be involved in His plan. God's scribes can have instructions for individuals, families, regions, nations, churches, corporations, government systems, and so on. There is a certain direction people or groups must go in to see the plans of heaven unfold. People remember and stay focused on what He says by way of writing the vision down.

Habakkuk 2:2 states, "Then the Lord answered me and said: "Write the vision And make it plain on tablets, That he may run who reads it" (NKJV). Without there being a vision written down, people have the propensity to perish. The people that are around you need to know where you all are going. You help people comprehend a piece of God's plan. This can be as simple as writing a vision down for your family. If you are an individual, you may write down a vision for your life or team. God can use you to write a book or teaching that delineates His vision for how to steward a certain part of their life. As God's writer, you have a strong desire to help everybody understand what God wants to do in the organizations that you are included in. You help create the culture or shift the culture of an environment by way of your writing. Your work can help a generation of people focus on the plans of heaven.

Chapter 3

Activations

There are certain activations or activities that can help prophetic scribes sharpen their writing gift. The following are eight ways to enhance or get your prophetic scribe writing gift started. Practice these activations as many times as possible to grow your prophetic writing gift.

Activation 1: Praying the scriptures.

Directions: Find a scripture that speaks to a certain situation that you are currently dealing with in this season of your life. Use the scriptures to create a prayer that can help you communicate with God about what you specifically need to move forward in your life.

Example: You may be dealing with a broken heart and disappointment.

A scripture that you can use to address this issue is Psalm 147:3 NKJV: He heals the brokenhearted and binds up their wounds.

Write out a prayer dealing with the brokenness and disappointment you are experiencing in your life.

Example prayer:

> Father, Your Word declares in Psalm 147:3 that You heal the brokenhearted and bind up their wounds. I bring to You all the broken pieces of my heart. I allow You to come into my heart to heal me of all brokenness that came in as a result of disappointment. I trust You to bind up every wound in my heart. Help me to learn how to move forward from what I thought life was supposed to look like. Help my expectations for people and opportunities to line up with the will of God. I will heal and move forward so that I can dominate in my destiny. In Jesus' name, I pray. Amen.

*Note: You can practice writing out as many prayers as possible. This is especially useful when you are experiencing immense anguish and do not want to verbally pray out loud. Writing out your prayers and saying them out loud can also help you grow in the area of prayer.

Activation 2: Prophetic Letters

Directions: Ask the Holy Spirit to give you a letter in the alphabet. Afterward, ask Him to show you a prophetic word or message using the letter that He gave you. Write out the prophetic word and allow Him to give you as many words that go with the letter that He gave you.

*Extra challenge: Try to time yourself to write for 5-10 minutes straight using the prophetic letter that He gives you.

Example: Letter A

As you **ASCEND** into more knowledge of your purpose and identity, you will **ANNIHILATE** the darkness, chains, curses that have been plaguing you, your family, and the people **AT-TACHED** to your purpose. Your **ASCENSION** into the truth of who you are will cause you to **AMEND** toxic relationships, habits, and thinking. Your **ATTENTION** to the things of God will liberate you and the people **ASSOCIATED** with your purpose. **ASCEND** into the real person that you were created to be, and embrace your idiosyncrasies so that you can make an **AMAZING** impact in your sphere of influence.

Activation 3: Healing Through Writing Letter or Poem

This is a longer activation that will require deep inner healing work. For the sake of this activation in this book, it will be abbreviated. Please make sure to get my other text *Healing Through Writing* to experience the full in-depth version of this work. There are 7 A's of healing that are discussed in that book. This prophetic activation deals with two A's- **address** and **aspirations.**

Directions: There are two parts to this activation. This activation involves choosing a painful moment that you want to address using writing. After you choose the moment that you want to address, you will have two options to address your pain in writing.

Part 1 Directions
Option A: Write a, "I AM SO ANGRY LETTER" to the person or situation.

18 · TOKUNBO O. OKULAJA

Option B: Write a poem that expresses your raw, honest emotions about how you feel about the situation. You can choose to use figurative language/imagery in your writing.

Part 1 Example: Angry Address (Option B)
depression & suicidal Thoughts are Like...

you're as loud as a teacher scratching her nails on a board.

you're as bewildering as a student loan payment.

you are as annoying as the wait in the DMV.

I want to fight you like my name is Mohammed Ali.

I want to shoot you to the ground,

I want to suffocate you like you have been doing to me all of my life.

Part 2 Directions
Aspiration- After you have expressed in writing some of the dark thoughts you have been holding in, the next part is writing out what aspirations God has for your life. Ask yourself: What hope do you have about the future after taking time to write? Who would you be if none of this stuff derailed you? Ask the Holy Spirit to show you what He has for your future. After you have completed writing down all the gloom and doom thoughts inside of your mind, you should start to aspire to see a better future for yourself. In this section, you will write another creative

A GUIDE FOR THE PROPHETIC SCRIBE · 19

piece, but this time this is your story of victory. You are going to speak prophetically about where you see yourself.

Similar to part 1, you can choose to write out a letter of hope or write a creative piece.

**Extra help: You can start your writing with, "I aspire to be" or ask God to give you one word to jump-start your writing.

Part 2 Example: Creative writing piece.

Delta
I aspire to be...

<u>Joyful</u>
Hopeful
Rule
Faithful
Irreplaceable
Full
Grateful
Wonderful
Plentiful
Relational
Thoughtful
Purposeful

Activation 4: Singing the Scriptures

Directions: Find a section of scriptures or one scripture in the Bible, and create a song using those scriptures. Be sure to create your own melody to go with the scriptures.

After you sing the scriptures, take 10 minutes to sit in silence to listen to what the Holy Spirit is trying to show you concerning the song and the scriptures you just sang with Him. Write out the message that He gave you for that one scripture.

***Extra challenge: After you write out the message that He gave you, sing the message out loud. Create a "song of the Lord" with the revelation that He gave you concerning these scriptures.

Activation 5: Meditate on One Scripture.

Directions: Find one scripture in the Bible that you want a deeper understanding of. Take 10 minutes or less to repeatedly read over that scripture. Afterward, take 10 or more minutes to write what the Master is showing you about yourself, family, or community using that scripture. Only focus on that one scripture. If God provides you other scriptures as you write about that one, write it down. The challenge here is to focus on receiving information from one scripture and to keep your pen moving for 10 minutes or more.

Activation 6: One Word or Picture.

Directions: Ask God to give you one word or one picture to write about. Ask Him the significance behind the word or picture. When you hear Him talking about the picture or word, write down the message. This message can be for you, friends, family, community, church, etc. Write down how this word or picture relates to who God is showing you.

Activation 7: Dream Chaser

Directions: Keep a journal of your dreams. Take time to write down a recent dream. Write down what you observed about this dream and then ask God to give you an interpretation of the dream. Write down what you feel He is saying to you about this particular dream.

***Extra challenge:** Write down the dream of a close friend or family member. Ask God to give you the understanding of the dream. First, write down your observations about the dream and then write down the interpretation of the dream. You can choose to share it with the person or not. Remember this is for your own personal practice to grow in your gift.

Activation 8: Ask God a Question.

Directions: One way to sharpen your prophetic scribe gift is by asking God one question at a time. After you ask Him this question, search for His voice for the answer. Have your journal or writing device out ready to write down what He has to say. (*Please note that God is sovereign; therefore, He can choose to deal with this question or highlight something else as you sit and wait on Him to speak.)

Question examples: If you are in a season of discovering your purpose in God, ask God the following questions listed below.

1. What have You called me to do? What is my purpose?
2. What is the problem in society that I was born to help humanity solve?
3. How will I serve, heal, and expand people in this world?
4. Who am I called to impact?
5. How do I currently feel about the purpose God has given me?
6. What next steps do I need to take now that God has revealed my purpose?

***Sentence Starters

There are different ways to start writing what God is showing you. Here are a few sentence starters to get your pen or fingers moving. You can use these sentence starters with any of the activations provided.

Sentence starters:
In this next season of your life…
In this next year…
I hear God saying to me….
I believe that God is saying…
I sense that God is doing…
I feel that God wants to…
I saw that God was…
I declare to you…
I prophesy that…
Daughter/Son, God is revealing
Dear_____,

Chapter 4

Growing Your Prophetic Scribe Gift

There are certain habits that all Spirit-led messengers must maintain in order to expand their reach as writers for the Holy Spirit. The following habits include Christian and practical disciplines that all Believers should frequently be doing in order to grow in their relationship with Christ. Ultimately, your intimacy with the Father will affect your ability to unlock mysteries from heaven. Revelation and insight on certain topics will not be something that you haphazardly stumble upon. God is going to challenge you in every season of your life to become more intentional about your growth and development in Him. If you have a gift from the Father that you want to see blossom, you are responsible to make the necessary financial and time investments to get educated on the topic. Proverbs 25:2 delineates that, "It is the glory of God to conceal a matter, But the glory of kings is to search out a matter" (NKJV). Your level of pursuit in the following areas is going to dictate the depth and weight of the words that you express. You have to spend time with the Lord in prayer, pray in tongues, study the scriptures, meditate on His Word, research the culture, spend time fasting, honor silence, and abide in love to grow your God-given skill.

Prayer and Devotion Time

All scribes that want to be used in greater ways should invest in spending quality time with the Father. Set a time to consistently meet with the Lord that works for your schedule. Ask the Holy Spirit what time you need to meet with Him to have your time of prayer. During this time of devotion, you spend time in prayer, worship, and listening. When you pray, you are having a conversation with your Father. You are leaving room for Him to speak to you as well. A teacher once said that the amount of time you spend talking should be the amount of time you spend listening to God.

Create time in your schedule to be intentional about spending time with your Father. This consistent devotion time will open you up to receive fresh manna from the Father's throne. God wants to spend time with you. Beyond only trying to grow your prophetic scribe gift, spending time with Jesus should be your highest priority as a Believer. This is the time when you learn more about the Father's nature and His heart for His people. When you are acquainted with God's nature, you have the ability to easily identify what He is doing in a certain season, region, year, and/or environment. This time of prayer will give you the necessary practice to learn how to hear straight from heaven.

Praying in the Spirit

To gain access to different facets of revelation from the Lord, it is important to take time to pray in your heavenly language. Some people call this praying in tongues. If you have been baptized in the Holy Spirit, you have the ability to receive the gift of praying in tongues. This is another way to pray and release the King's agenda into the earth. If you have not received the ability to pray in tongues, ask the Holy Spirit to fill you up. Keep asking,

A GUIDE FOR THE PROPHETIC SCRIBE · 25

seeking, and knocking at His door if the gift does not seem to manifest the first time around. If you want a fresh way of speaking in tongues, you can always ask the Holy Spirit to fill you up with new tongues.

We are strengthened in our understanding of the Lord and how He operates by way of us using our prayer language. Jude 1:20 expresses, "But you, dear friends, by building yourselves up in your most holy faith and praying in the Holy Spirit..." (NKJV). If you want to grow in hearing God's voice, you must practice praying in the Holy Spirit. This gift that has been given to you directly connects you to God. He understands what you are saying to Him when you pray in your heavenly language. Sometimes, you pray in tongues because, in your native language, you do not have the ability to pray the exact ideas that God wants to build on the earth. Our human minds do not have the capacity to know what we should always pray for. Praying in the spirit gives God access to show us what our finite human minds cannot ask to see. God can pray a perfect message through you if you use praying in tongues. Praying in tongues can help you stay connected to the heart of God.

In addition, you have the ability to ask your Creator what He is revealing to you by way of you praying in the spirit. Paul shares in 1 Corinthians 14:2, "For he who speaks in a tongue does not speak to men but to God, for no one understands him; however, in the spirit he speaks mysteries." The King knows what you are saying. As you pray in the spirit, allow the Holy Spirit to reveal what it is that He is trying to show you. Paul lets us know in 1 Corinthians 14:13 that you should pray to get the interpretation of what you are praying about to the Father. Use what He is unveiling to you to write out a prophetic announcement for the audience that you are called to impact.

Challenge yourself to pray in the spirit as much as possible in a day. When you first start out, pray in your heavenly language for 15 minutes a day. As you continue to receive more downloads, you should desire to pray in the spirit for 30 minutes or more a day. Wherever you are, whenever you can, pray in the spirit. Paul emphatically champions the ability to pray in tongues. He states in 1 Corinthians 14:4, "I wish you all spoke with tongues, but even more that you prophesied; for he who prophesies is greater than he who speaks with tongues, unless indeed he interprets, that the church may receive edification" (NKJV). He goes on to say in verse 18, "I thank my God I speak with tongues more than you all..." Spiritual growth can transpire as a result of praying in the Spirit. Apostle Paul understood the benefits of praying in the Spirit because that was his direct connection to hear the heart, mind, and will of the King. Our prophetic gifts can be sharpened because of our consistency in using our prayer language.

Study the Scriptures

As was mentioned earlier, being a heavenly wordsmith means that you have to understand God's heart for His people. You understand His heart, nature, and character by way of becoming intimately acquainted with the Scriptures. The Bible gives you direct access to hear the voice of the Father. Scripture tells you that you must study the Word of God. (See 2 Timothy 2:15) Studying the Scriptures is going to allow you to understand how the Lord flows with His prophetic scribes. Reading the scriptures helps you to learn the type of tone that the Father would have with His children. Reading the Bible gives you insight into the symbols and expressions that the Father would use to convey a message to His children. Hearing God's tone, nature, and character are areas that you learn more about as you read the Bible.

You can receive more revelation based on your level of study. You can expect to find treasures about the King by diving deep into the scriptures. Studying goes beyond casually reading the text. Those that study the text want to know how these words correlate back to knowing the heart of Jesus. When you study the text, you get into the details of definitions, geography, history, and so forth.

If you do not have a study life, it will be difficult for you to speak for God on a sturdy foundation. Everything that you do and say must have a biblical foundation. Messengers are enlightened and inspired because of the scriptures. Take an assessment of your relationship with the scriptures. Have you made biblical truths the center of everything that you do in your personal life? When the Bible guides your decisions in life, it will be displayed in the work that you have been designed to create.

Meditate on the Word

Meditation is a daily practice or habit that all prophetic scribes need to adopt to be a writer that carries depth. According to Webster's Dictionary meditate means to, "focus one's thoughts on, to reflect on, to muse, to mull over or to ponder over and calls for a definite focusing of one's thoughts on something so as to understand it deeply."[1] Concentrating on a certain scripture for a set time in a day is going to give you the ability to hear ample revelation from the same scripture. Challenge yourself as a prophetic scribe to ruminate or ponder on the same scripture for weeks. When you read this scripture, ask God to show you new ideas based on that one scripture. There is so much revelation, meat, and wisdom that can be extracted from reading one scripture.

Joshua 1:8 is the scripture that encourages us to be a meditator of God's word. It states, "This Book of the Law shall not depart from your mouth, but you shall meditate in it day and night, that you may observe to do according to all that is written in it. For then you will make your way prosperous, and then you will have good success." The Hebrew word for meditate in Joshua 1:8 is hagah. The strong's exhaustive concordance states that hagah means to moan, growl, utter, speak, muse. It means to imagine, mourn, mutter, roar, sore, speak, study.[2] The word meditate is a verb that connotes action or participation. Meditation demands that you are an active participant in the digestion of the scriptures. This means that you go beyond sitting in church to only listen to the Bible when your pastor teaches or preaches. Meditation requires you to take ownership over rewiring your brain to think like God through the meditation of His Word. When you think like God, you can write what He wants to share with His people.

Research and Cultural Competence

There is a specific audience that you are called to impact. With that being said, there is a specific jargon that this group of people understand. It is your responsibility to, first of all, know what audience you are called to impact. When you know that information, you study the concepts and ideologies that this group of people can discern.

Jesus used symbols and sayings in His parables that were culturally relevant to the Jewish people of that time. He knew that there were certain ideas that Jewish people could relate to that could lead to a deeper understanding of His teachings. You may not know the significance of certain protocols in scripture because you may not have grown up under Jewish culture and traditions. As a prophetic scribe that is called to a certain age or epoch, you have to do research on the dialect and traditions that your audience can relate to. You have to use concepts in your writing that will get your audience to accurately discern what it is God wants them to know to live fruitful lives.

Oftentimes, God may give you certain words, pictures, or concepts to write about that you may have never heard of before that day. When He does that, He is inviting you on a journey to unpack revelation on this topic that will help this generation and the one to come to praise His works. Prophetic scribes have to be people that enjoy research. After you have studied your Bible, there are certain literature, classes, and teachings outside of the Bible that you need to invest in to learn more about a topic. If you are called to speak to doctors, you would certainly have to do research to understand the rhetoric that doctors use to be able to reach them. Do not be afraid of going back to school, watching tutorials online, and/or investing in a program that will help with your gift. The investment that you put in to investigate more about a subject area God is calling you to will be what causes God to be able to expand your reach. It is acceptable to be biblically literate and culturally competent.

Spend Time Fasting

As a Believer, you should cultivate a lifestyle of fasting. A biblical perspective of fasting means abstaining from food. When you decide to abstain from food, this is an act of worship. Jesus mentioned in Matthew 6:16 that He had expectations for all of us to fast in our Christian walk. Fasting gives you the ability to invest more time in your relationship with God. The time that you could have spent cooking meals and eating is replaced with increased times of devotion. These times of devotion are made for you to fellowship with the Creator who gave you your talents.

Fasting also gives you an opportunity to learn how you can become more like Jesus. As a representative or an ambassador for Christ, His main focus is that you are formed in His likeness and image. If God wants to use your voice in greater dimensions, He desires for you to live like Him. Your message can go further when you continue to evolve into looking more like Jesus. Fasting gives you the chance to see where it is that you still need healing and cleansing so that you can look more like the King.

Furthermore, fasting teaches you how to not gratify your selfish ambitions. It is important to be a person who does not gratify your selfish ambitions because representatives of Christ should learn how to use self-control with their gifts. There are moments where the King will want you to keep silent, and there are moments where He will command you to speak. Fasting gives you the ability to learn how to be led by the Spirit when using your gift. Allow fasting to purify you and teach you self-control so that you can be a vessel of honor.

If you have any medical issues, ask your doctor how to approach biblical fasting. While you are fasting, you can drink water and/or 100% juice. Be careful not to eat heavy foods when breaking a prolonged fast. You can choose to abstain from food from 9-5, 6-6, 24-hours, or a set number of consecutive days (7 days, 10 days, 21 days, etc.). Beyond prolonged fasts, choose certain days of the week to fast. Try to incorporate intermittent fasting in your days as well. Intermittent fasting involves choosing set times to eat in the day. Ask the Lord what kind of fast He wants you to devote to Him. Seek the Lord to figure out how He can challenge you to do something different in your lifestyle of fasting. Ultimately, the Master can tell you what you are capable of accomplishing.

In addition, you can choose to fast from watching TV, listening to music, going to your favorite places, eating your favorite foods, etc. Choose to fast from something that will cost you your comfort. There are so many sacrifices that you can make to help you grow closer to God. The goal of fasting is to seek greater time with the Father and to be open to hearing how He wants to transform you. As you change in Him, your gift can evolve for the better. During a time of fasting and afterward, expect that the Father will provide you with fresh ideas on how to use the skill that He has given you. When you first start out, it will be difficult, but you will see the benefits of fasting as you chase after Jesus.

Silence and Journaling

Prophetic scribes need to value times of silence. It is in these times that you can hear God speak to you. While you are silent, you can concentrate on scripture or take the time to journal what you sense God is saying to you. He is not always going to immediately speak when you ask Him a question. It will be your level of pursuit that keeps you waiting on Him to hear what the King of kings has to say.

Spending time in silence can mean that you journal what He wants to say to you for that day. In general, you should push yourself to journal for at least 10-15 minutes a day if you want to grow your writing gift. Ask God a question. When you ask Him a question, have confidence that He will answer you. Show Him that you expect Him to speak by having your journal, computer, or notebook out ready to record what He has to express.

Challenge yourself to go with the flow. Your aim is not to be perfect, but to be led by Him.

Abide in Love

Love should be the ultimate reason that you want to share your gift with others. Gifts were meant to be shared with other people. Your gift does not belong to you, but it is for the people that have been placed around you. It is a requirement to use your gift from a place of love. Scripture makes it clear that you can prophesy as much as you want, but if you do not have love, you have nothing. (See 1 Corinthians 13)

You are going to grow exponentially when you abide in love. Abiding in love is going to be the greatest key to getting you to reach new heights with your gifts. Going to classes, practicing your gift, reading books, etc. will all mean nothing if you do not steep yourself into understanding true agape love. Study what agape means. Practice loving the unlovable. Embrace times when you are in situations with difficult personalities. These are the moments where God is welcoming you to grow in love. You are a more trustworthy messenger when you give the King access to enhance your love walk.

Do not allow yourself to be so puffed up that you hear from God that you forget to use your gift from a place of love. All of the messages that you give people should be rooted in love because God is love. You use your gift because you want people to know that God loves them. When you genuinely love His people, He can trust you with more messages and influence. As you grow in love, the Master can grow your prophetic gift.

If you are having a difficult time loving the people that are being sent to you or writing out the work that God has given you, ask Him to shed more love in your heart for His people. (See Romans 5:5) Ask Him to help you see people around you through the eyes of love. Allow the Holy Spirit to help you not see people's sin, but to see them the way He sees them. Give the Lord the ability to teach you how to not be easily offended and angry with others. When you grow in love, you can create straight from the heart of the Father. Lives are transformed because you gave out messages or created work from a place of love.

Chapter 5

Prophetic Scribe Protocol

There are certain protocols and standards that prophetic scribes should adhere to when it comes to sharing their work with other people. Wordsmiths commissioned by heaven have to responsibly use their power. One of the ways that you can responsibly use your gift is by healing in private but sharing wisdom in public. Also, you have to discern when it is best to share your work with others. Prophetic scribes know that it is important to use the linguistics of heaven to carry out His message. Beginning prophetic scribes seek out wise counsel before sharing personal prophecies with people. Lastly, God's messengers are trusted to handle certain messages with confidentiality.

Heal in Private

As was mentioned earlier, you may be a prophetic scribe because you carry the gift of healing through your pen. You have experienced healing through writing in God's presence. There are certain words you have written in your journal that were meant for your own personal deliverance. It is noble to share your honest story with others, but you have to be wise on what to share with your audience. As a Spirit-led scribe, do not only share your story on brokenness with your audience. If you do not have wisdom attached to your story of pain, then you should not share your story in writing with others. In addition, there are parts of your deliverance journey that others do not need to know. A teacher once mentioned that writers must discern if they are writing for their own deliverance. When you are done writing a vulnerable and transparent work, ask yourself: Did I write this for my personal deliverance, or did I write this to help others to heal? People cannot handle the weightiness of the agony that you have experienced. When you write, you can sometimes overshare in your writing. Oversharing can lead to overwhelming readers.

Furthermore, there are certain things that we write that come from dark places. When you have not healed or you do not have a great perspective about your story, you can share too much darkness with your audience. You want people to be liberated with your words. You do not want more heaviness (sadness) or confusion to come to the individuals that participate in reading your art.

Writing is a great way to heal and express your emotions. There is great revelation and wisdom that you can be extracted from the Holy Spirit's heart when you take time to heal through writing. It is the wisdom and jewels that the Father wants you to expound upon to your audience. Figure out how to balance sharing your pain, but also sharing wisdom in the work that God gives you to present. It is great to share your story so that your audience can connect with you. As you create, keep in mind that you should share your story of redemption and hope so that you can motivate others to heal from their pain.

Discernment Through Prayer

Not everything you write down needs to be shared with others. This is especially important if you are a scribe that writes down messages about certain people. There are times when

God may have you write down a message so that you can pray about the situation. Prophetic scribes have a unique relationship with the Lord where He wants some ideas to only be between you and Him. Oftentimes, you can get discouraged because you shared information that was never meant to be broadcasted with a group of people or a person. You may be excited about what has been shown to you in your private time, but the people that read it may not experience the same joy. There are times that this happens because it may not have been time to share this message or you shared it with the wrong people.

Take time to pray about the messages that are revealed to you before you share them with other people. Ask Him if this message was given to you to only pray about or share with a particular person. There are certain times and seasons where the people you are called to can handle what it is that you are trying to show them. Other times, the Lord may simply want to share something with you so that you can pray about a situation. Regardless, every message that God gives you is an opportunity to pray with Him about what He has given you.

Linguistics from Heaven

There are times when the Holy Spirit will show you a term or concept that you may not fully comprehend at the moment. It is not your job to change the word or repudiate the concept because you do not understand what He said. Take time to research the word or idea that He has given you before you disavow the information. The people that you are writing for have to hear certain terminology for them to grasp what God is showing them. These ideas may be peculiar to you, but they are significant for your audience. You may not fully understand what it is, but God knows the heart of the people that He wants to reach. Trust Him with concepts that may seem enigmatic to you. Again, when new terminology or beliefs come to your mind, it is an invitation from heaven to get you to go deeper with Him.

Remind yourself of how many times the Holy Spirit told you to say or write something, but you didn't. You may have been too fearful or distracted to document or speak about this topic. Later on, you hear that same message or word that God was trying to get you to use. These words also could have been the information that someone else may have needed to hear at the moment, but you allowed yourself to get in the way of partnering with the plans of your Father. When these moments arise, your response is usually: I was just going to say that, or I was thinking about saying those words! Ask yourself: Why didn't you use the words the Holy Spirit showed you? What scares you from using the terminology that He wants to share with His people? What has deciding to not move when God speaks cost you and others that are connected to you? Other people are affected when you decide to not use what God has given you to its fullness. Do your diligence as a prophetic scribe to research the ideas that He is showing you. Work hard at not downplaying the message that God has given you to present to His people. What may seem peculiar to you could be the very concept that helps free another person. The Father knows what His people need to hear more than you; He is methodical and intentional with His language.

Safety in Counsel

If you are a novice or beginner at using prophecy, ask the Holy Spirit for a prophetic mentor to help you as you use your gift. If you have written out a prophetic word for a specific person that you may not have a close relationship with, it is wise to share your writing with a prophetic mentor who has more wisdom than you. Share what you wrote with this trusted leader in your life. See if this leader can hear God's heart in the message

A GUIDE FOR THE PROPHETIC SCRIBE · 37

that you have written out. Also, ask this trusted guide if it is appropriate to share this message with the person that you want to give it to.

Before sharing the message with the person you wrote it for, you should ask the Lord for the perfect timing to share it. If He desires for you to share the message, it will keep coming back to your remembrance. If you feel a burning desire to share this message you have written for another person, it is wise to bring a witness to listen to you read the message. Also, if you scribed out the message, provide the person with the message, and record who was there when you delivered the message. You should also put a time stamp on the note.

Following this protocol does not mean that the person will or will not receive the message that you have written. If you feel peace to share it with the person after sitting with the message for a while, then you need to have joy that you did what God told you to do. In addition, you should not be looking for any rewards or satisfaction from man when you deliver a prophetic written message.

There are times when a message from God is urgent. In this case, you will not have time to speak to a mentor; therefore, go with the leading of God. If the message is urgent, and you have confidence that He has sent you, deliver the message in love. If you do not feel God's peace after delivering a message, seek His face to understand why. Ask Him to show you why you have not experienced peace. Do not beat yourself up if the other person did not receive the message. Simply ask God where you need to grow in the area of prophecy. You may have had a message straight from God, but you lack peace because you are more invested in having man's approval. Invite God in to help you have peace after you convey His words.

Confidentiality

If the Lord does give you a message for a specific person, you should keep it between the people that were there when it was read. The person who received the message can decide to share it with others if he or she wants to share it. Do not discuss the details of the message without receiving permission from the person who received the writing. Again, you only contact the trusted leader when you are unsure about a message or you are a beginner at delivering messages to people. After you share the message, you should not continue to discuss the details outside of that context.

Keep conversations about prophetic messages specifically for people between you and God. If you want to share your experience about using the gift, leave people's names and intimate details out of your testimony. It can be difficult to keep certain messages to yourself because of excitement or worries. Discuss with God your worries and/or excitement about the message that you gave the person.

Chapter 6

Increasing Your Creative Intelligence

There are certain habits that you need to adopt or investments that you need to make to increase your creative intelligence. You will not grow tired of your prophetic scribe gift if you are continuously removing limitations off of your creativity. All ingenuity belongs to the Father. He allows you to think in ways that give Him the ability to express Himself throughout the world. Spirit-led authors can increase their creative intelligence by way of investing in education, traveling the world, listening to mentors, befriending other creatives, and journaling with God.

Investing in Education

There are courses and degrees that you can take to expand your thinking about a subject area. Listening to teachers and being surrounded by other students that have a wealth of information can spark a new interest for you. Going to school or investing in a class opens up the opportunity for you to learn more about an idea that you did not understand. You may have some wisdom on a subject, but investing in your education should add new insight to what you already know. The assignments and opportunities that teachers expose you to can help generate new schools of thought and shift your thinking.

Investing in your education does not always mean earning a degree. Discover the online courses, certification programs, workshops, etc that you need to enroll in to get a better understanding of your area of choice. Be strategic about where you need to place the most energy so that you can gain more wisdom on a particular subject. Take the time to research the people that you need to be partnered with to help elevate your creative intelligence.

Traveling the World

Earlier, it was discussed that you should practice being culturally competent. You become culturally competent by learning about people from different cultures. You can learn about different cultures and people by taking the time to travel the world. When you travel the world, allow yourself to get to know the people that are from that specific area. Be open-minded to learn about a way of life that may be different from your own.

It is important to meet people that have different backgrounds and cultures than you because they help you think about life from an unexplored perspective. You may not know about an issue that plagues a certain group of people because you never learned about this people group. There are various thoughts and problems that people have in certain communities that you will not know about unless you visit these places. There is also a beauty about different people's cultures that will help you have more information to continue to be a creative prophetic scribe.

If you cannot physically go somewhere, you can always travel the world via the Internet. Learn about a culture that can help influence the type of work that you create. Learning about a different community allows you to create new forms of thoughts that can help increase what you can write about for God. You will never run out of ideas to write about if you allow your perspectives to be widened from learning about people from all over the world.

Watching and Listening to Coaches and/or Mentors

One of the ways that you are inspired to continue to produce work is by surrounding yourself with coaches or mentors who motivate you to do more. You should have at least one close mentor that has done more than you that gives you the belief that you can dream bigger. Elohim can use you to push limitations when you are a person that is not afraid of dreaming.

You may have trusted voices in your life that you do not have a personal relationship with, but you are inspired to learn from them through their teaching, books, programs, lifestyle, and/or preaching. These are the coaches or mentors that teach you from a distance. You listen intently to what has made them successful, and you learn how to modify their principles to fit your unique life. In essence, you are not only a hearer of what they have to say, but you put their words to action. It is also best to note that you should not listen to too many voices because that will confuse you. Be strategic about the voices that you listen to in each season of your life. Choose four areas that you want to grow in, in one year. After that, find out the leading voices in those areas, and study their books and teachings as it relates to your goals for the year. Be strategic and intentional about who you decide to mentor you. Their ability to speak into your area of growth can help elevate your thinking and innovative brilliance.

Befriending Other Creatives

Being around other individuals that want to build something bigger than themselves should inspire you to create. As a Christian, you can learn from unbelievers if they inspire you to push creative boundaries. Obviously, you should know when an unbeliever is giving you information contradictory to the Bible, that you should discard that information. Do not limit yourself to being around the same type of people. When you are surrounded by other dreamers and thinkers, it should help you become a critical thinker. You start to think about how to build worlds and systems that have never been created because of other people motivating you to dream greater.

In addition, you should also try to get in rooms with people who have way more wisdom than you. Creatives that have accomplished more than you should cause you to want to work harder to see what else can be achieved through you. Instead of people being jealous of others, people should start to normalize asking people to help them sharpen their craft. When you are inspired by someone, ask them: How did you do that? How did you accomplish this goal? One answer from someone that knows more than you can catapult you to years worth of success.

When you are surrounded by genius minds, you are challenged to not be a lackadaisical thinker. Being in the same room as other creatives should ignite a new passion and hunger inside of you to create. You do not know all that you need to know for where you are about to go. These people may be different than you, but they may be the key to helping you unlock your destiny. Be humble enough to learn from all types of people. He will place people in your pathway to enlighten you to think differently. There are people that will expose you to terminology, concepts, and vantage points that you never considered. Instead of being intimidated by the brilliance of others, use that as the fuel to expect to see more of the Father's glory. Surround yourself with people who inspire you to create something that the world has never seen before.

Explore the Mind of Your Father

Take time out of your structured journaling time to write down visions and dreams from the Father. Have Him show you the many ways that He wants to use you. It is great to go on a "mind exploration" with Him to hear ideas from His viewpoint. Ask yourself this question from time to time: If money was not your concern, what would you do with your life? Ask the Holy Spirit to show you visions and dreams He has for your life. How does He plan to use you to help other people? Give Him access to your mind to leave you speechless and in awe of His presence.

The Father will show you the unconventional mechanisms that He will use to display His glory through your life. It is your duty to seek the Lord on how He can use your entire life to manifest Himself on this earth. If what He is showing you is bigger than yourself, then you can believe that it is a God-sized dream. Journal with God to have Him show you His God-sized dreams for your life. These colossal visions involve many other people being impacted. In addition, you will know this is a dream from the Creator because the idea will take a team of people to help bring this vision to life. You will know that it is a heavenly idea because it is something that you could have never thought of on your own. This vision should motivate you to keep completing work for Him.

Find different times throughout the year to simply explore the mind of the Lord. When you dream with the Creator of the entire universe, there is no need to write anything perfect. Allow your pen to freely move so that He can show You a frontier that He wants you to explore. Let your imagination be free in the presence of a holy Being.

Chapter 7

Prophetic Scribe Roadblocks

There are roadblocks or impediments that come to hinder you from finishing the work that you were created to produce. Be aware of these hindrances in your life that will derail you from being fully used by God to write out His messages. Most of these hindrances are internal battles. You will know that you are suffering internally if it hinders your ability to concentrate and produce with your Father. These internal battles affect your ability to consistently think about whatever is noble and true. It affects you from living in spiritual freedom with God. Every person deals with these internal issues, but it is a serious problem that needs your attention when it is consistent and affects your quality of work. Deal with internal issues such as pride, excessive worrying, writer's block, procrastination, and the spirit of heaviness. When you deal with the root cause of these issues, you can continue your work of being a prophetic scribe.

Lack of Humility

It is exhilarating to be used by the Lord. If you continue to write for God and share it with people, individuals can begin to praise you for your writing work. Scribes for God need to be reminded that all the glory needs to go back to the One who gave it to them. In 1 Peter 5:5, we are warned here, "God resists the proud, But gives grace to the humble" (NKJV). This same message is repeated in James 4:6. Humility is a monumental principle that needs to be inscribed on the hearts of His people. Pride has caused a lot of people to stumble from the reason why they first got involved in doing the work that was given to them. Once you stray away from the fact that the King deserves all the glory, it will lead you down a path far away from holiness.

You stick close to your Father by way of humility. You can be used in a powerful way because of your meek heart and disposition towards the King's will. Prophetic scribes are trusted with weighty messages because of their level of humility. Apostle Paul was a man that was full of great revelation. His life consistently taught us that walking in lowliness was what kept Him close to the Lord; humility is what gave Apostle Paul access to explain mysteries about Christ. In 2 Corinthians 12, Apostle Paul teaches us that though he experienced many great visions, he did not want to boast about the lofty visions that were revealed to him. Specifically, in 2 Corinthians 12:6, he says, "For though I might desire to boast, I will not be a fool; for I will speak the truth. But I refrain, lest anyone should think of me above what he sees me to be or hears from me." He goes on to explain in that chapter about a "thorn" that was given to him to keep him humble. He teaches here that people should not think more highly of themselves than is necessary because of the gifts or opportunities that God has given to them. All the creativity, wisdom, talents, and opportunities that you possess are only because God chooses to share them with you. Maintain a posture of humility so that in due season God can raise you up. (1 Peter 5:6)

*Here is a declaration for you to say to keep your heart humble in the sight of the Father. Make it personal for you.

Repent and ask the Holy Spirit to show you the root cause of pride.

> **Say:** Father, I repent for showing any haughtiness as a representative of Christ. Forgive me for being prideful when using or not using the gifts that You have given me. Help me to see the root cause of pride. Remind me that none of my wisdom, talent, education, and gifts belong to me. You are the One that provides me with revelation.
>
> I desire to see Your name glorified in my life. The same declaration that John the Baptist made in John 3:30 is my heart's cry. I want You to increase, and I want to decrease. I make a declaration that my heart posture will remain low even when you elevate and expose me to the world. I ask You to help me to humble myself under the mighty hand of God and help me to wait on You to be the one that lifts me up according to what Your word says in 1 Peter 5:6. Also, let the words of my mouth and the meditation of my heart be acceptable in Your sight according to Psalm 19:14. I need You to help shape my thoughts so that I can remain humble before You, Lord.
>
> In Jesus' name, I pray. Amen.

Overthinking, Worry (Fear), and Anxiety

As a creative, you can oftentimes worry yourself out of being obedient to the Master. Unfortunately, when you fill your mind with overthinking and excessive worrying, it takes up mental space in your mind. Instead of using this cognitive space to think creatively and produce, you use this storage to obsess about concepts in life that you cannot control. When you overthink, it hinders your ability to move into execution and originality.

Satan is not intimidated because you are gifted. He is not intimidated because you hear God and can write. The enemy is intimidated by you when you take what the Lord has given you and decide to execute His plans. When you move into execution mode, it gives other people the ability to be blessed by your gift. When you decide to take action, it causes other people's faith to rise. Living out your God-given destiny is a point of contact or a reference point to give others the belief that their heaven-inspired dreams can come true.

Overthinking and excessive worrying puts you in a place to not create and write. Allow the Master to help you stop overthinking every single detail of your life. Invite your Father in your thoughts to help release you from obsessing over the worst-case scenarios. While you are worrying about details, God has already figured them out for you before even one day came to be. (Psalm 139:16)

*Say this prayer out loud to deal with excessive worrying and overthinking. Make this prayer personal for you. Allow the Holy Spirit to reveal to you the root cause of overthinking, excessive worrying, fear, and anxiety. Where did it come from and what has it cost you?

Say: Father, in the name of Jesus, I repent for overthinking and worrying about details in my life. I ask that You would reveal to me where this spirit of fear has come from. Why do I spend so much time worrying rather than believing You for good outcomes?

Your Word declares in Psalm 139:16 that every day of my life was ordained before even one came to be. I trust You with the days and details of my life. Help me to stop overthinking about things that I cannot control. Help me to learn how to cast my anxieties on You because You care for me. (1 Peter 5:7) I decree and declare that I am anxious for nothing. I decree and declare that I will learn how to turn my anxieties over to you by praying with thanksgiving and supplication.

In Jesus' name, I pray. Amen.

Writer's Block

There are so many gifted writers that will not write because of experiencing writer's block. Again, once you deal with your mindsets, you can overcome experiencing writer's block on a consistent basis. Being a prophetic scribe is a gift from the King. You should be able to write at any moment, whether it be a piece that is short or long. If you feel that you are experiencing immense hardships to get motivated to write, try the four ideas listed below.

Find a new writing environment. There are times when a new writing environment will spark new ideas. If you are not able to write at home, go outside. Go to a place where you feel the most peace and comfort. Find spaces that you believe are aesthetically pleasing. You can also surround yourself in coffee shops or offices with other creatives who are working on certain projects. There are times when you need to be in an environment that is full of productivity so that it can inspire you to keep creating.

Rest. Take a few hours or days to rest your mind. Come back to your writing project with a refreshed and rejuvenated mind. Do not take too long to come back to the writing project because it will be difficult to get back into your writing momentum.

Let it flow. There are times when you do not know how words are going to sound together; therefore, you decide to not write. You may not have all the pieces about what you want to write, but it is best to simply start writing. When you start to write, believe that in the writing process things will start to make sense.

Pray. Ask the Holy Spirit for new ideas to add to your writing. Afterward, take 10-15 minutes to sit in silence to receive those new ideas.

*Here is a prayer for you to say to overcome writer's block. Whenever you are experiencing barriers to your creative flow, begin to pray.

Say: Father, in the name of Jesus, I break off any lies that have intimidated me from continuing to write for Your glory. I command myself to not capitulate to strange voices that tell me that I do not have great ideas. I will be a listener and doer of what You tell me to write. I will believe that You have given me the ability to write for Your glory. I stand on what Your Word says in John 10:27. I am Your sheep; I hear Your voice, and I will continue to follow Your lead.

I ask that You give me creative ideas from heaven. My mind is submitted to you to receive knowledge and wisdom from the King's throne. I am free to create with my Master.

In Jesus' name, I pray. Amen.

Procrastination and Inconsistency

There are larger writing projects that the Father may give you as an author, producer, and/or creative. When you are given these larger writing projects, you have to keep at the forefront of your mind that this is a mandate from heaven. If there is a book, screenplay, curriculum, manual, or blog post series that God needs you to produce, procrastination cannot stand in your way. Procrastination can oftentimes lead to inconsistency. Lacking consistency will hinder you from receiving more projects from the Lord to complete. Also, others may not want to work with you if you have shown yourself to be inconsistent. You need people to partner with you to bring heavenly dreams to life. The Creator is looking to give out information to those who are able to follow through.

In addition, assignments from the King mean that they are time-sensitive. There are people that need to hear your message at a specific time in their life. Take God's deadline seriously when it comes to following through on the mandate that He has given you to execute.

The list below is three ways to overcome procrastination.

Self-awareness. You have to have awareness and accept the fact that procrastination is causing you to have issues with your ability to produce. Ask the Holy Spirit to reveal to you the root cause of why you procrastinate. There can be many reasons including, fear, fear of failure, fear of success, self-sabotage, perfectionism, doubt, overthinking, and so forth.

What is your "why?" You have to ask yourself: Who or what is going to be negatively impacted if I do not write what the Holy Spirit is showing me? Who is going to suffer as a result of me sitting on my gifts? You need to have a reason for completing what God has given you. Your writing is bigger than you. Your why, mission, or vision is going to give you the fuel you need to stop procrastinating.

Make new confessions. Oftentimes people say that they work better at the last minute because they can feel the pressure. In reality, more fine-tuning could have been done if a project was started on time. The King wants His work done in excellence. Eliminate saying: I work better under pressure, or I work better at the last minute. Start to say: I will start working on projects early. Say that you will no longer live your life in delay. Make a new confession that you will work at optimal capacity by starting new projects on time. What you say about yourself is how you will behave. You may not change overnight, but keep repeating to yourself that it is mandatory for you to no longer live a life of procrastination.

*Say this prayer out loud concerning procrastination. Also, allow the Father to highlight to you why you lack consistency.

Say: Father, in the name of Jesus, help me to discover the root cause of procrastination in my life. Show me why I deal with inconsistency. Reveal to me the opportunities that I have missed out on because of procrastination and inconsistency. I repent for allowing fear, (insert your root cause), (insert your root cause) to keep me in a state of delay. Help me to have the same urgency that You have about my assignment on the earth.

Teach me how to become a better steward over the time and days that you have given me. Teach me to number my days so that I may gain a heart of wisdom. (See Psalm 90:12) Help me to believe that I can finish work on time. Place me around people who follow through on their goals. Show me the importance of finishing and starting on time. Help me to no longer take for granted that You have chosen me to partner with You to build Your plans on the earth. Thank You for trusting me.

In Jesus' name, I pray. Amen.

Dealing with the Spirit of Heaviness

A lot of the issues mentioned including overthinking, fear, writer's block, and procrastination can be a result of not managing your emotions well. Emotions can get damaged when you avoid dealing with the spirit of heaviness. The spirit of heaviness can come in your life as a result of experiencing traumatic events that led to immense agony. The spirit of heaviness may show up in the form of consistent despair, grief, depression, suicidal ideation, self-pity, doubt, and isolation. When the spirit of heaviness is a large part of your life, it can make it difficult to produce. You will know that this is a hindrance for you because you will lack the passion to create the art heaven has given you.

The spirit of heaviness is more so inward-facing. When you deal with the spirit of heaviness, you are more self-absorbed; therefore, you are not thinking about how you can help other people. When other people are not on your mind, you will not feel the urgency to move on the visions given to you.

Be honest with the Lord and trusted leaders about any heaviness and depression that you are experiencing in life. Get the help that you need through prayer, deliverance, inner healing, and therapy so that you do not sit on the gifts the Creator has given you. There are professionals out there that are willing to help you safely unpack the pain that has left you stagnant. Let trusted family members, friends, mentors, counselors, and advisors around you know that you need help. If you have been trying to be free on your own, chances are you are still strug-gling. Allow your Father to show you what life will be like for you on the other side of the pain.

The spirit of heaviness creeps in the hearts of God's scribes to deter them from focusing on the assignment in front of them. Whatever word curses or lies that you have believed about yourself need to be addressed. Allow your Father to focus you on the truth so that you can continue to keep His people's eyes on His promises.

*Say this prayer concerning the spirit of heaviness and depression. Allow God to reveal to you where this spirit has come from and how it has affected your creative abilities.

Say: Father, in the name of Jesus, I come out of agree-ment with being partnered with the spirit of heaviness. Today, I repent for trying to work out the issues of depres-sion, suicidal thoughts, (insert personal struggle) on my own. I repent for trying to hide depression, suicidal thoughts, (insert your own personal struggle) from people who love me. Today, I rebuke the thoughts, the lies that say I do not need any help to deal with depression, sui-cidal thoughts, (insert your struggle). I cast down the lies that tell me that I am fine staying broken.

I renounce any ties with an independent spirit. I come out of agreement with trying to fight by myself. I break all gen-erational curses in my bloodline of keeping secrets and seeking ungodly counsel. I close the open doors and gen-erational patterns of keeping secrets and having an independent spirit. Being emotionally unintelligent will no longer be part of my story and legacy. Through my Father, I have the ability, courage, and strength to be transparent and vulnerable to those that will not mishandle my story.

A GUIDE FOR THE PROPHETIC SCRIBE · 55

Father, I ask that You will reveal to me the people in my life that I can trust to help pray for me and encourage me during this time in my life. Please show me the counselor or therapist that I need to partner with in order to deal with my painful past. You said in all of Your ways acknowledge Him and He will make your paths straight. I acknowledge that I need Your help to seek counseling for depression, suicidal thoughts, (insert any other struggle).

I command that I will be liberated from the spirit of heaviness. The spirits that come with heaviness are no longer allowed to live in this temple. Holy Spirit fill me up right now with righteousness, joy, and peace in the Holy Spirit (Romans 14:17).

In Jesus' name, I pray. Amen.

Chapter 8

Hardships of a Prophetic Scribe

There are hardships that you may have to go through as a prophetic writer. The tribulations that you endure are intended to bring glory to the Father. If you despise the journey that you are on, you may not receive wisdom from these seasons. When you do not have the wisdom to share with others, it is difficult to lead people to a place of victory. There are adversities that you will overcome that you did not necessarily cause yourself. God will allow you to experience certain things so that you can write from a place of compassion.

Prophetic scribes may have to live out a message before they write about it. (Read Hosea's story.) They will also be tested by their own words after they have finished a writing assignment. In addition, prophetic scribes can be woken up at unusual hours to write down a message from God. Lastly, you can grapple with a topic with God for a while before you receive ample information on what it is that He wants you to write.

You Lived the Message

There are times when you will experience pain and suffering so that you can write from the perspective of someone that has been through what he or she is writing about. You can write with love and compassion towards others when you have been through the same trials. There are parts of your story that you wish you could erase from your life because it was so painful. Ask the Lord to give you what it is He wants you to write concerning that issue. You will find that sharing about the situation can provide you with another layer of healing.

There is beauty in your story. What you have gone through was painful, but you can turn it into something beautiful by helping others to heal. You turn ashes into beauty when you use your voice to go back to help someone else prosper from painful experiences. Take control of the narrative by reminding yourself that you are not what happened to you. Prosper from painful experiences by telling the world that you lived to tell the story from a place of victory.

Practice What You Teach

Oftentimes, people quit writing in the middle of an assignment because they realize that if they write something they have to practice what they write. The words that you write will convict you. This is normal because it is the Holy Spirit that has the power to convict people. It is the Holy Spirit that gives you the inspiration to write; therefore, you should be convicted by the words that you type. Do not be surprised when the words that you typed out come back to test you.

Do not be afraid to continue to type because you believe that you have a hard message. Trust God to write out a good message that will help others, but also trust Him to give you the grace to live out this message. Prophetic scribes have the responsibility to continue to do the inner work necessary to practice what they teach in their writings. Give yourself the grace to continue to evolve in the area that you are teaching or writing about. Being the writer does not mean that you have it all together. You are writing because you were chosen. Rely on the Holy Spirit to help you deal with any other inadequacies that you have about being the messenger.

In addition, be motivated to write what has helped you. Write what has helped you personally transform your own life. You may not be fully where you want to be, but you know that there is something that has been given to you that can get people started on their journey. You are a much more powerful prophetic scribe when you disseminate wisdom that has personally changed your life.

Wake Up, God Wants to Speak

There are moments where you will get inundated with information from heaven at an unusual time of the day. Similar to prayer, God can wake you up at whatever time He desires so that you can get directions on finishing a writing project. Take advantage of those moments because you never know when He is going to allow these divine appointments to come back. Late nights or early mornings may be idyllic for God to speak to you because it is quiet. This is a time where He may have your full attention. When you hear words, messages, and themes replay in your mind at these different times, take out your computer to record what He is sharing. Ride the revelation wave when He visits you.

There can be times when you feel melancholy or too exhausted to create, but you feel the Father tugging on you to produce. Your mind will say no, but your spirit will leap because you sense the Creator opening up new information to you from His chambers. When these strong creative urges emerge, go with the leading of the Father. You will know that this is a tug from heaven because you will receive downloads and visions that only heaven could have shown you. Heaven will start to bombard you with wisdom that you did not understand before. Do not limit yourself to only creating when you feel like it or when you think the timing is best. Sometimes you do not create because you think your surroundings have to look a certain way. Do not allow your need to be comfortable to override accomplishing divine work. It may not be comfortable or the right time for you, but it is the time that has been appointed by heaven.

Wrestle with God

There are topics, ideas, or concepts that are not going to be handed to you in one sitting. It may take a while to understand the fullness of what God wants to show you. You may start studying something with God now that will not get used until a later time in life. If God gave you this insight, hold the information close to you because it will make sense later on.

In Exodus 23:30, God teaches Moses about the principle of little by little. The Holy Spirit may give you pieces little by little to avoid overwhelming you. You may get discouraged when you do not understand the greater picture and if you cannot currently make sense of what He is showing you. Think of this as an opportunity to grow in the gift of faith. In addition, getting to the larger picture requires that you have the puzzle pieces. At the appropriate time, if you keep chasing after the Lord, He will give you access to the greater plan using prior seasons puzzle pieces. Your Father knows how much information you can handle at every point of your life. Don't give up on the journey God has given you because the pieces you have do not currently make sense to you.

How far are you willing to go to receive more jewels from God? You can be required to go on a fast or focus your studies on one subject so that you can learn more about the spirit realm.

Proverbs 25:2 says, "It is the glory of God to conceal a matter, But the glory of kings is to search out a matter" (NKJV). Pursue God for answers. Consistently look to Him for what you want to know.

Depending upon the nature of the subject and your commitment level, it can take you weeks, months, or years until you get the principles that are necessary to help transform other people's lives. People need you to write principles that will lead them closer to Jesus. Wrestle with Him until He releases the wisdom that will cause people to live victorious lives in Christ Jesus.

Do not allow frustration or impatience to cause you to abandon your studies. When you get frustrated, keep asking questions. Keep bombarding heaven until you see a flow of information. The Lord is trying to create a seeker out of you. As a prophetic scribe, you can never grow tired of pursuing God. Your seek life is going to give you the ability to have more information to share with His people. You will feel a sense of relief and joy when you finish writing what God has given you to share with your audience.

Chapter 9

27 Prophetic Scribe Declarations

This chapter is full of declarations to speak over yourself as you evolve in your prophetic scribe gift. Declare these over yourself as often as possible. When you feel weary, make a declaration. Whenever you lack creativity, make a declaration. In the end, create your own declarations that will help you stay consistent and grow in your prophetic scribe gift. Declare them over you as you embark on new projects with the Creator.

1. My writing gift is making room for me in uncommon places.
2. My writing gift will give me access to stand before great men. (Proverbs 18:16)
3. I will continue to become skillful in my work so I can stand before kings. (Proverbs 22:29).
4. My voice will travel all over the world by way of my writing gift. (Mark 16:15)
5. I have the creative intelligence to build something that the world has never seen before. (1 Corinthians 2:9)
6. My words will be used to change the world.
7. My words have the ability to bring healing, hope, and strength to my audience.
8. My pen is my sword.
9. My words bring deliverance and freedom to my audience.

64 · TOKUNBO O. OKULAJA

10. God, You can use my voice, pen, hands, and words to turn the world upside down. (Acts 17:6)
11. My tongue is the pen of a skillful writer. (Psalm 45:1)
12. I seek God for the linguistics of heaven. (Jeremiah 33:3)
13. I will boldly declare the Word of the Lord to His people. (Psalm 28:1)
14. I am disciplined to dominate in my destiny.
15. I will help the next generation praise the work of God's hands by way of my writing gift. (Psalm 145:4-5)
16. I am a king/queen that deeply searches out a matter in God. (Proverbs 25:2)
17. I acknowledge God in all of my writing endeavors. He is the One that leads me. (Proverbs 3:5-6)
18. I am like the sons of Issachar because I understand times and seasons. I can skillfully communicate times and seasons to other people. (1 Chronicles 12:32)
19. I will help abolish the evil in my community by way of my writing gift.
20. I will help people discover their identity, purpose, and destiny in God by way of my prophetic scribe gift.
21. I am called to restore communities by way of rhetoric.
22. I will use my voice to bring God's plans into the earth.
23. I will focus people on the plans that God has for their life. (Jeremiah 29:11)
24. I write God's vision down. I make the vision plain so that others may run with the vision. (Habakkuk 2:2)
25. I will not be ashamed of proclaiming the Gospel into the world. (Romans 1:16)
26. I will not grow familiar with my writing gift. I allow myself to evolve as a writer in all seasons of my life.
27. God will use my words to write screenplays, scripts, plays, commercials, poetry, books, curriculum, podcast

series, articles, and more that will help bring glory to His name. (Matthew 5:14)

*Write out your declarations that deal with the dreams that you have about where God is taking you and your writing gift.

Encouragement for Prophetic Scribes

This book was written to help you take your prophetic scribe gift seriously, upgrade your skill set, and explore with God where He wants to take you. As a Believer, you do not have to limit yourself to using your gift only in the Church. Find out where God has called you. Define with Him where He wants you to share your gift with others. There is so much that God can do through you if you understand the power of rhetoric.

What commercials, songs, screenplays, books, plays, etc. have you always wanted to create? All of these ideas start with conveying a message through language. Discover what area God has called you to dominate. Where He has assigned you is where you will make the most impact.

If you put down your pen because of hurtful words a teacher, family member, mentor, friend, or stranger said to you, then I want to encourage you to forgive them so that you can be free. These hurtful words may have caused you to suffer from self-doubt and shame. Do not allow hurtful words from the past to dictate where God wants you to go. The enemy may have detected at an early age that you are full of brilliance. He probably saw it before you did. He made sure to squelch your desire to write so that you would live as the inauthentic version of yourself. The enemy is so committed to evil that he decided to use anyone around you to discourage you from using your gift.

Make the enemy furious by deciding to use your art to liberate people that are still in darkness. You will win when you embrace the truth that greater is He that is within you than he that is within the world. (1 John 4:4)

If you feel that there are not a lot of people that look like you writing about what you create, then be the representation that the world needs. Disrupt the system and challenge stereotypes.

People may have mocked you in the past because of your interests, but this can be the very idea that inspires other people to create.

I encourage you to forge forward when you feel the enemy resisting you or you experience hardships. Even though you may receive specific instructions to create certain art, it does not always mean that it will be an easy journey for you. Again, the enemy is indignant that you have embraced your idiosyncrasies and have decided to take action. There are going to be distractions and challenging moments. When these moments arise, allow the gift of faith to grow inside of you. When difficult times come, discover how resilience, bravery, and chutzpah are being formed in your DNA. Allow any journey that the Lord takes you on to draw you closer to Him so that you can create from His perspective. Also, remember that spiritual interference may come because there will be many testimonies of how your work helped set people on the right trajectory.

Partner with God to use your superpower. Your superpower is that your words seep into the heart of people to make them believe in a God that is full of wonder and splendor. You are not an ordinary artist. You are a vessel of honor chosen before creation to boldly proclaim: Thus saith the Lord!

Notes

Chapter 4

1. "Meditation." Merriam-Webster.com Dictionary, Merriam-Webster, https://www.merriam-webster.com/dictionary/meditation. Accessed 23 Jan. 2022.
2. "H1897 - hāḡâ - Strong's Hebrew Lexicon (nkjv)." Blue Letter Bible. Web. Accessed 23 Jan. 2022.

About the Author

Tokunbo Okulaja is a first-generation American born to Nigerian parents. She grew up both in Prince George's County Maryland and Fairfax, Virginia. She graduated with a Bachelor of Arts degree in Government and Politics with a minor in Rhetoric from the University of Maryland, College Park. Tokunbo Okulaja also completed her Master of Arts degree in Public School Building Leadership from Teachers College, Columbia University in New York.

In 2013, Tokunbo joined Teach For America. This began her ongoing career in teaching middle school English, language arts, reading, social studies, and leadership in both public and charter school settings. Tokunbo served as a lead teacher in underserved communities in Mississippi, Louisiana, Illinois, and North Carolina for seven years. Because of her dedication to developing young leaders, she became the founder of Redeem the Teens Global Ministries. Their first initiative is the When Gentlemen Speak program, where they focus on equipping young, Black males to excel in academics, character, and entrepreneurship.

In 2019, Tokunbo became the CEO and founder of Tokunbo The Leader LLC. Tokunbo The Leader LLC is designed to help leaders discover VIP (Voice, Identity, and Purpose) so that they can dominate in their destiny! She currently resides in North Carolina where she continues blazing trails in the area of education.

Learn More at tokunbotheleader.com!

Stay connected with Tokunbo and learn how to use your writing and leadership gift by reading blogs, receiving updates on courses, and so much more!

Tokunbo The Leader
tokunbotheleader
Tokunbo The Leader

Made in the USA
Columbia, SC
28 October 2022

70093255R00046